T0065473

Endorsements for
Arrows Make Terrible Crowns

The circle that encompasses 'Godly Moms' is
a lot bigger than I originally thought. I realized I'm
included in the circle I tend to excuse myself from.

  - Ambri Heimerman - mother of four

In reading *Arrows Make Terrible Crowns*, I felt
challenged and motivated to love my children with
God's grace. I really like the opportunities Janet
gives with the questions and opportunities to write
things down. It was really good how she brought
up to look at the relationship with your own mom.
So good and important.

  - Courtney Bullard - mother, founder and
    executive director The Pearl House
    www.thepearlhouse.org

Janet gives biblical wisdom to moms who want
to be a godly parent, comfortable in their skin. I
highly recommend *Arrows Make Terrible Crowns* for
any parent who struggles to guide their children
into God's best for them and his kingdom.

  - Rev. Jonathan Srock, M.Div. - author, teacher
    www.jonathansrock.com

Janet writes with disarming vulnerability and invites mothers to engage in an exploration that many mothers feel too guilty to touch. I look forward to recommending this important book to some of my clients.

- Jonathan Stube, Ph.D, LPC

This book is a fresh invitation to get honest about motherhood and to surrender to God's design. Janet Mylin has a gift for transparency and relatability. She's that mom-friend who can celebrate your greatest success and shoulder your greatest trial. I'm glad I took my time with Janet's insights, writing prompts, and questions - they were keys that unlocked deep places in my heart that needed healing. Plan on being loved and healed by God as you read *Arrows Make Terrible Crowns*.

- Laura Booz - mother, writer, speaker
  www.laurabooz.com

I love your artistic yet very authentic style. I also love how you leave space, literally, for the reader to be engaged and work through their own junk.

- Jarrod Sechler - father, teacher, pastor

Arrows Make Terrible Crowns

How the Holy Spirit healed my view of motherhood

Janet Mylin

WESTBOW
PRESS®
A DIVISION OF THOMAS NELSON
& ZONDERVAN

WestBow Press books may be ordered through booksellers or by contacting:

WestBow Press
A Division of Thomas Nelson & Zondervan
1663 Liberty Drive
Bloomington, IN 47403
www.westbowpress.com
844-714-3454

Because of the dynamic nature of the Internet, any web addresses or
links contained in this book may have changed since publication and
may no longer be valid. The views expressed in this work are solely those
of the author and do not necessarily reflect the views of the publisher,
and the publisher hereby disclaims any responsibility for them.

Any people depicted in stock imagery provided by Getty Images are models,
and such images are being used for illustrative purposes only.
Certain stock imagery © Getty Images.

Scripture quotations are from the ESV® Bible (The Holy Bible, English
Standard Version®), copyright © 2001 by Crossway, a publishing ministry
of Good News Publishers. Used by permission. All rights reserved.

ISBN: 978-1-6642-1775-1 (sc)
ISBN: 978-1-6642-1776-8 (e)

Library of Congress Control Number: 2020926010

Print information available on the last page.

WestBow Press rev. date: 03/09/2021

For Beth Appleton and Sue Margolis

You don't know each other and might never meet.

But in Heaven someday, you need to sit down and compare notes.

Beth, you taught me the power of transparency and grace.

Sue, you taught me the power of prayer and replacing lies with Biblical truth.

Contents

What does that symbol mean?

One day I had an image pop into my head. Through the beauty of being married to a graphic designer, Andy and I created this image.

The arrow is representative of a child, as referenced in Psalm 127:4-5, which you'll read more about in The Arrow section of the book.

The crown is representative of our identity in the Lord. God is the King of all the earth (Psalm 47:7). We are His adopted children, heirs and co-heirs with Christ (Romans 8:15-17). We are royalty.

When we launch our children out into the world as weapons against the kingdom of darkness (Ephesians 6:12), we need to do it THROUGH our own identity in Christ. Our confidence in God and who He created us to be is the very guide we use in order to release our children to be used by Him.

And, incidentally, arrows make *terrible* crowns.

I have been lots of different types of moms...

Mom of a son

Mom of a daughter

Public school mom

Private school mom

Homeschool mom

Hippy school mom

Cyber school mom

Adoptive mom

Internationally adoptive mom

Older child adoptive mom

Mom of a child with physical special needs

Mom of a child with psychological special needs

Mom of a child with emotional special needs

Stay at home mom

Working outside of the home mom

Traveling working mom

Working from home mom

Entrepreneur mom

Adult child mom

Mom of a high honors child

Mom of a child in Special Education classes

Mom who's experienced miscarriage

Mom of an athlete

Mom of an artist

Mom of a musician

Mom of a verbal processor

Mom of a quiet processor

Mom in poverty

Mom in wealth

Mom who chooses gentleness

Mom who chooses the immediate release that comes with rage

Joyful mom

Depressed mom

Peaceful mom

Anxiety-ridden mom

Mom who draws their child close

Mom who pushes their child far, far away

Mom who stays

Mom who runs

Spineless mom

Warrior mother

I have been a lot of different types of moms.

And I love the type of mom you are.

PART ONE

The Holy Spirit

CHAPTER 1
The Cups

You know how some dates are just marks on the calendar, and then something happens on that very average date, forever changing it to **A Date I'll Never Forget**?

June 4, 2018 The day God gently told me I needed to "invite the crushing" so my life could be poured out. Just like the bread and the wine of Communion, grain and grapes are multiplied through the crushing. Naively, but trusting, I said, *"Lord, if You are the One who is doing the crushing, then yes. I invite it because I invite You."*

July 4, 2018 I saw my mom for the first time in a couple years. There was brokenness in our relationship. I wanted to take a step towards reconciliation and I think she did, too. Our reunion wasn't magical, but I was encouraged. Maybe we could move forward?

July 6, 2018 My mom's spirit very unexpectedly slipped away from her wing-back chair and joined the unbroken presence of her Perfect Father God.

Thus began a season of crushing I could never have imagined. Loss, sickness, more loss, pain, hard goodbyes, depression. For months.

In the midst of mourning the loss of my mom, the loss of opportunity for reconciliation, the loss of expectancy, I've done a lot of deep work - with counselors, the Lord, the Word, my journal, and some trusted individuals. As I've processed my relationship with my mom, it helps me to picture this:

> I picture my mom's dresser in her bedroom. All lined up with cups. Not physical cups. Figurative cups - all of them representing good things that she wanted to pour into me. Some of them were empty because she gave them to me. But others were full. Full of things she wanted to give me but, for some reason, didn't or maybe couldn't.

But the cups. They were there. Probably my whole life. She wanted to put those cups to my lips in life but *just couldn't do it*.

And then I thought of all moms. *I thought of me.*

Don't we all have cups of good things we want to give our kids? Cups of courage, strength, love, grace, joy, discernment, purpose. But shame can keep us from thinking we have the authority to give them to our kids if we aren't drinking from them ourselves. Or maybe it's inadequacy. "I don't know the first thing about joy. Obviously. So what makes me think I can help my kids drink from a Joy Cup?"

I'm thinking about Rahab from the Bible. She was a prostitute. She had zero percent of a reason to trust *any* man. But she willingly entered into a trust contract with two spies from Joshua's army, literally putting her life and the lives of her family members in their hands. She didn't drink Trust along with her coffee in the morning. But she found it within herself to pick it up anyway in order to protect her family from imminent destruction. (You can read the whole story in Joshua 2-6.)

You may be thinking, "What did she have to lose? Her city was going to be destroyed anyway." True. But she took a risk for the sake of freedom. Freedom for herself and freedom for the ones she loved the most.

Are you willing to take that risk?

My friend Chizzy, born of a Nigerian woman who came to the motherhood table with entirely empty hands, always reminds me of this: "Girls do not have to see something modeled by their mother in order to do it." She speaks of her mother's utter dependence on the Lord to equip her as a mother, raising her four children in His ways, His love and His faithfulness alongside her God-fearing husband. Chizzy's mom literally had no other resource to learn Biblical motherhood except for the Lord!

Because of the Holy Spirit, we are not empty-handed. No matter what our past looks like or doesn't look like, we have a Helper, an Advocate and a Comforter to help us pick up cups we've never even touched before so our kids can have a drink.

Do you have any thoughts you want to write down after reading this?

Take this space to do that now.

CHAPTER 2
Spirit, Teach Me

My greatest breakthrough in motherhood began several years ago. Why did I need a breakthrough? Good question.

I have struggled deeply in my role as a mom. That doesn't mean I don't love my children. Of course I do. (Although, I don't always *like* them. And I know they don't always like me. Can I get an Amen?) But when I dove into mothering, I felt like I didn't know what to do with myself. Let me re-write that: I didn't know what to do with my Self.

Was this all I was supposed to do?

I don't like playing with them. Is that terrible?

When they make bad choices, does that prove I'm failing at momming?

Yelling at my kids feels like such a release in the moment, but that's terrible, right?

I want to do some other things, but I always get interrupted by their needs.

How can I possibly be a woman after God when I can't seem to spend any concentrated time in the Bible and prayer?

Why do those other women seem to absolutely thrive as moms?

Why can't I just joyfully put my Self aside like those other moms do?

Why am I not consistently happy to spend time with my kids?

Is this all there is for me?

These years of pouring into them seem like wasted time for me.

What is motherhood supposed to be anyway?

Does the Bible even have actual help for moms?

Are the marks of a virtuous woman found in Proverbs 31 all I have for my instruction?

I thought I needed to become the kind of mom my critical, comparing mind concocted. If I could have replaced myself with the cultural conglomeration of what I thought a mom should be, I would have. But God didn't want that for me. And He doesn't want it for you either.

I ended up at a women's conference, not expecting to get much out of it, to be honest. Afterwards, I found myself speaking to one of the women who gave a testimony of healing and wholeness in her life. At one point, she looked at me and issued a challenge: **Spend time just focusing on intimacy with the Holy Spirit.** She thought this would somehow begin to heal my view of motherhood.

At that point in my life, I was climbing around on the nets and ropes of anxiety - especially in the area of motherhood. I was desperate for freedom and I didn't see how intimacy with the Holy Spirit was going to change anything, honestly. But, because I love a challenge, I immediately went on a secluded walk with my codependent Miniature Schnauzer, Poncho, and started talking to the Holy Spirit.

At first it was awkward. I was being very...polite. I was like, "Thank You for always being there. You're so great. I'm glad You're in me..." It was so flat...like my hair after I got baptized in the 80's. But then, I started getting real.

> *I see Your activity in my life, but I'm not sure I trust You.*
>
> *Do You just use me to make You look better?*
>
> *Do You actually know me or do You just appease me?*
>
> *I see You doing lots of cool things, but I don't think I trust Your motives.*

Me and Poncho. Me drowning in a sea of tears. Poncho padding along, stopping when I needed to. Moving when I was ready to move again.

That day I realized I had a broken view of the Holy Spirit and that needed to change. So, where did I logically go? The Bible. I found all kinds of verses about the Holy Spirit's purpose and attributes. In John 14 alone, we learn the Holy Spirit is our Helper, Counselor, Comforter, Advocate, Teacher, and our Reminder (verse 26).

In other portions of scripture, we see more of what the Spirit does. This is by no means an all-inclusive list, but you'll get a good feel for things.

The Spirit convicts us of sin. (John 16:8)

The Spirit renews us. (Titus 3:4-7)

The Spirit helps us in our weakness and intercedes for us. (Romans 8:26-27)

The Spirit seals us. (Ephesians 1:13-14)

The Spirit gives us gifts. (1 Corinthians 12:7-11)

The Spirit guides us into truth. (John 16:13)

The Spirit empowers us. (Acts 1:8)

The Spirit frees us. (2 Corinthians 3:17-18)

The more I learned about this seemingly mystical person of the Trinity, I kept seeing the same thing over and over.

The Holy Spirit is a perfect Nurturer.

In John 14:16, Jesus refers to the Spirit as a Helper. "Parakletos" is the original Greek word used here. The embodiment of its definition is "to come alongside." That's right. The Holy Spirit comes alongside us. How beautifully, *perfectly* nurturing.

Always present. Helping. Counseling. Giving. Truth-speaking. Keeping us in check.

Just like the role of a mother. A healthy, whole mother.

Listen up: I AM NOT PROCLAIMING THE HOLY SPIRIT IS A WOMAN. NOR AM I PROCLAIMING THAT THE HOLY SPIRIT IS OUR "HEAVENLY MOTHER."

I *am* saying that for the first time in my life as a mom, I felt truly seen in the pages of my Bible. I now had a powerful role model in the area of nurturing, helping and advocating.

And then a simple prayer: "Holy Spirit, since You are the perfect nurturer and helper, I am asking You to teach me about motherhood."

And so it began.

I determined to ask and keep asking the Spirit to mentor me. I intentionally read scripture with "motherhood eyes." Every time something came up in my mind that seemed a wrong definition or view of motherhood, I pressed into it, asking the Spirit to replace it with God's truth.

And the book that follows contains my biggest takeaways from that season.

If you're realizing your view of the Spirit needs to change, hang tight. We'll get there.

PART TWO

The
Arrow

CHAPTER 3
My Sad Crown

I had read it lots of times.

> *Like arrows in the hands of a warrior are the children of one's youth. Blessed is the man who fills his quiver with them! He shall not be put to shame when he speaks with his enemies in the gate.*
> PSALM 127:4-5

Okay. So children are like arrows. That's nice.

The words of this Psalm weren't new or even unexpected. I found myself reading that Psalm for no particular reason, other than getting some of God's Word into my brain.

And then He interrupted me. God whispered a statement that would make this familiar scripture highly disruptive to my everyday life.

"Janet, arrows make *terrible* crowns."

What? I'm wearing my children like a crown for *myself*?

I've seen this over and over when I look at myself and other moms, an unhealthy mindset of "my child's behavior is the source of my honor." If my child isn't "doing well," I can't feel good about myself. This can leave us running around life constantly breaking our arrows, gluing them and forming them into some sort of crown for ourselves.

But arrows make terrible crowns.

Maybe it would look cool at first glance, but the fact remains: Those arrows were meant for something else.

This begs the question, what *are* arrows good for?

When I asked a group of teenagers (aka: "arrows") this question, one girl very matter-of-factly said, "Arrows are for stabbing someone from a distance." Hmm. Yep. That pretty much sums it up.

In the context of scripture, the "someone" these arrows are meant to "stab from a distance" is the Enemy of our souls. Satan, to be specific, and all of his works and workers.

If you're not familiar with Ephesians 6:12, you might want to cozy up to it a little bit. It will sustain you, especially when you think your *child* is the enemy of your soul, not the Devil. Here's what it says:

> *For we do not wrestle against flesh and blood, but against the rulers, against the authorities, against the cosmic powers over this present darkness, against the spiritual forces of evil in the heavenly places.*
> EPHESIANS 6:12

Our children, when launched out into the world, are meant to do damage to the kingdom of darkness.

They are...

Lie busters

Darkness illuminators

Confusion clarifiers

Truth speakers

Freedom fighters

And we can be very afraid to let that happen. Well, at least I can. What about you?

Stop for a minute and answer this question:

What is it about launching your children out into the world that scares you?

I thought it was easier to just *not* launch them out - to save them (and me) from pain.

CHAPTER 4
Broken Arrows

Let's go over two specific ways we can use our arrows incorrectly.

We break our arrows.

As we've already discussed, we can take our arrows, break them and keep them as a crown for ourselves. How does that look in real life? Well, for me on a real regular basis, it would look like this:

> *You need to clean your room.*
>
> *You call this a clean room? Do it better.*
>
> *There's still stuff under your bed. Do you think I'm stupid and can't see it?*
>
> *Why can't you put your pants away? I've made this as easy as possible for you and you STILL can't seem to do it!*
>
> *Forget it. Just leave. I'll clean your room because I can't handle it looking like this. I have all this other stuff to do but now I have to clean your room. This is ridiculous.*

The child is in tears and I'm storming through the room in a tirade of contempt - hating myself and relishing the control all at the same time.

Honestly, my old companion Shame is knocking on my door after writing that. I'm embarrassed to even share it.

I would break the child's freedom to do things imperfectly in order to make myself feel better. Broken arrow. Ugly crown.

Another example of breaking the arrow might go something like this:

You have a high schooler who's had a desire to go to other countries since she came out of the womb. An opportunity comes up for her to go to a country in Africa for a week with people you know and trust.

But.

What if something happens to her? What if she gets sick? What if she gets lost? What if the plane crashes? What if terrorists attack? What if, what if, what if... all of them landing on "I couldn't deal with that."

And you say "No." Not out of wisdom. Not because the Lord directed you. But out of fear.

Arrow broken. A crown of safety for yourself.

The reason we do this is because we have a hard time trusting God with our children. It's hard to believe He will show up for our kids in their struggle. Or at least we think we'd do a better job of taking care of them.

I truly believe one definition of Anxiety is imagining a future that is absent of God's grace and love. There may be some exceptions to this, but I haven't found one in my own life yet. If I'm breaking my arrows out of fear, it's because I really don't believe God is FOR them or WITH them - not now and not in the future.

What if instead of breaking the arrows to become our adornment, we focus on firmly planting ourselves in Christ SO THAT our identity becomes the vehicle we use to launch them out into the world? What if, instead of breaking our arrows, we launch our kids strategically THROUGH our own unshakeable identity in Christ?

I am convinced this is how the Proverbs 31 woman can laugh without fear of the future in verse 25. It's because of the piece before it: *She is clothed with strength and dignity.* A woman clothed in strength and dignity isn't walking around in insecurity and fear.

Did your parents or guardians fearlessly launch you out into the world? If so, how?

What are some areas in which you felt broken by your parents? For instance, were you a natural artist, but your parents pushed you towards a non-creative field? Did you have dreams, but your parents' negativity paralyzed you?

If you have children, in what ways are you tempted to break your own arrows, either out of fear or out of control?

Take a few minutes now, or make time later, and talk this through with the Lord. Even if you can only focus on it for three minutes, do it. It's not about the time as much as it's about your heart. Do you have a trusted friend or mentor who can hear the answers to those questions without judging you? Set a time to do just that.

CHAPTER 5
Rejected Arrows

We shoot the arrows away as a defense mechanism.

This is my personal go-to.

There are times when I've needed to separate myself from my kids in order to cool down or, quite frankly, not hit them out of anger, either with my hands or my words.

Maybe you've done this, too.

Take a deep breath.

Talk yourself down from the ledge.

Pray.

Get your pulse rate down.

Look at the situation with the eyes of a cool-headed adult, not a crazy woman who suddenly decides she hates everything and everyone forever.

That always seems to be a wise decision, although, admittedly, I've often chosen to just go with my raging emotions instead of taking a minute to get my cool back. Grace is a beautiful thing.

But sometimes, I would frantically separate my kids from me in order to just not have to deal with them, help them, talk to them, focus on me, whatever. I'm not talking about getting some healthy "me time." I'm talking about getting them out of your face in order to not have to deal with them at a time when you know they need you.

This is what I would do:

I would grab that arrow, stick it in my bow and just shoot it away from me. It didn't really matter where it landed. *I just needed the arrow to go away.*

To their room.

To a babysitter.

To the TV.

To anywhere but here.

I've found when I disconnect myself emotionally, even if the kids are right in front of me, it's the same thing as shooting them away from me. In both instances, I am removing their right to be in my space.

I've heard it said the moments you want to disconnect from your kids the most are the very moments you need to pull them in close.

Why is that so hard sometimes?

After talking to friends, and from my own experience, it seems how we were raised has a ton to do with it. I've composed a list of some good questions to guide you as you think through this. I use your mom in the questions, but feel free to apply it to your dad, caregiver, a coach, a teacher or guardian.

When you did something wrong or annoying, how did your mom respond?

Does she still operate in that way?

How do you think that has affected the way you act and react with your kids?

Here's something else I have seen.

Sometimes what looks like shooting our arrows away, isn't that at all.

I've seen friends who have particularly difficult situations with their older children get to a point of letting them go. It's not an act of exasperation, but more of an intentional "giving them over" to figure out the potential pain of their trajectory.

Psalm 81:10 says, "Open your mouth wide, and I will fill it." Every parent can relate to this plea, can't we? If they would just listen to us, we could save them from so much pain. But Israel wouldn't listen and they didn't want God around. Verse 12 tells us God "...gave them over to their stubborn hearts, to follow their own counsels."

My friends who've had to do this released their children in a similar way, trusting that their child would be drawn back into the Father's arms, and, hopefully, their arms as well. I don't see this as shooting their kids out into dark places. I see it more as an act of tucking their arrow back into the quiver under a covering of intercession and trust in God. They didn't shoot their children out anywhere. They chose to pour themselves into prayer and trust.

CHAPTER 6
Redeemed Arrows

Don't be discouraged. No matter what you're feeling right now, don't give up. No matter how many connections you've made between your current life and your past life, it's not too late.

The devil's job isn't that hard. Truly, all he has to do sometimes is plant the seed of a tiny lie in my mind. And then I take the seed and nurture it until it becomes a huge debilitating force in my life.

Do you know what this does? It accomplishes one of the enemy's primary goals for humans: It paralyzes me.

If he can't kill me, he will do everything he can to stop me from doing anything good.

It makes me think about Job in the Bible.

I don't understand the ins and outs of this story, but it begins with a conversation between God and Satan. Satan tells God that he's been "roaming throughout the earth."

Let's pause there for a second because that reminds me of another verse. 1 Peter 5:8 says: "Be sober-minded; be watchful. Your adversary the devil prowls around like a roaring lion, seeking someone to devour."

It is safe to say that when Satan told God he's been roaming the earth, Satan was looking for someone to devour.

So God gives him someone.

WHAT?!?

> *Have you considered my servant Job? There is none like him on the earth, a blameless and upright man, who fears God and turns away from evil.*
> JOB 1:8

After a second encounter, God tells Satan he can do anything he wants to Job, except he can't take Job's life (Job 2:6).

As the story goes, Job literally has everything taken from him. All of his wealth, his children, his health. His wife looks at him and encourages him to just give up on everything. Give up on God and everything (Job 2:9).

Pause for a moment. Are you in a similar mindset right now? Do you find yourself at a crossroads of "Give up" and "Press on"?

What helps you persevere in the tasks God has placed in front of you?

Job lost almost *everything*. His life looked like a wasteland of hopelessness from the onlooker's point of view. It seemed impossible that he wouldn't die alone, poor and discouraged.

After Elihu comes on the scene in chapter 32 and rebukes Job and his three friends who were not pointing him towards hope in the Lord, things shift. Because Job and God had a pretty lengthy discussion. Rather, God spoke truth and Job mostly listened and repented.

What did Job's repentance and confession produce?

> *And the Lord blessed the latter days of Job*
> *more than his beginning.*
> JOB 42:12

I know we're mostly talking about motherhood here, but think of any area of your life in which you feel fruitless or useless. Repent of any specific thing the Spirit brings to your mind. Then ask God to bless your latter days even more than your beginning days.

Here's some space for you to write or draw that out.

In the name of Jesus, let's believe God has the power to transform a life so much that our latter days are even greater than our beginning days! It is not too late for the Lord to instruct you in the ways of a powerful, warrior, archer mother. Just humbly submit yourself to His teaching and pursue what He places in front of you.

In speaking with a group of moms I love and adore, one of them expressed with raw honesty the negative narrative she speaks over herself as a mother. Her words conveyed a sense of **"I don't see how I could ever change. How could I ever get better?"**

It made me think.

I don't believe it's true. Not that I don't believe her struggle is real and sometimes debilitating. But I don't believe she is truly hopeless, as if there's nothing more for her. Do you know why? Because I know she pursues God. When she's able, she dives into scripture and chews on it like it's her job.

Because she believes there's more.

That's why we pursue wholeness, intimacy with God, and His voice. If we didn't believe there was more than what we're currently experiencing, there wouldn't be much of a reason to nurture our relationship with God. As followers of Christ, carriers of the precious Holy Spirit, we are always drawn towards more. Eternity is set in our hearts (Ecclesiastes 3:11). We are continually, gloriously haunted by a draw towards more.

If we're in a dry, hard place, we pursue God because we know there's more. We know God provides the nourishment and growth we need. He is the place of lasting change and wholeness.

Let's pray this prayer of David:

> *O God, you are my God;*
> *earnestly I seek you;*
> *my soul thirsts for you;*
> *my flesh faints for you,*
> *as in a dry and weary land*
> *where there is no water.*
> PSALM 63:1

CHAPTER 7
Launching Arrows

Okay. We know our children are like arrows. But the question remains: How do we launch them? I'm not an expert, but I can tell you how we do it with our kids. Specifically, I can tell how about how this looked with Lucy, our oldest. She graciously gave me full permission to share all of these stories with you.

1. Set the Arrow
Connect with their strengths and passions.

Story Time:

My dad travels all around the world encouraging native missionaries and pastors as they do the hard work of sharing the Gospel in their land. Lucy was a very little girl, like toddler aged, and she watched my dad's VERY long slideshow of his first trip to India. She was seemingly riveted while some of the other grandchildren ran around or left the room.

After that, she said, "I want to do what Papa does!"

1 Samuel 16:7 is my favorite verse. I guess you could call it my life verse.

> *But the Lord said to Samuel, "Do not look on his appearance or on the height of his stature, because I have rejected him. For the Lord sees not as man sees: man looks on the outward appearance, but the Lord looks on the heart."*
> 1 SAMUEL 16:7

We could have looked at Lucy watching those slides and thought, "Isn't she cute? She loves to look at pictures of different looking people." But instead, we allowed God to open our eyes to see what He saw: her heart. There was a passion developing inside of her but we had to choose to see it. **Setting the arrow looked a lot like setting our eyes on the gifts we saw in her and helping her connect with those gifts**.

2. Aim the Arrow
Set them on a trajectory.

Story Time:

As I was sweeping the floor about 5 or 6 years ago, God interrupted my thoughts with this statement, "It's getting to be time for Lucy to be exposed to extreme poverty." Once I realized He wasn't talking about our family's financial condition, I told my husband, Andy and we knew to keep our eyes open for that opportunity. We didn't tell Lucy. We just prayed and kept our eyes open. It wasn't too long before we were sitting in church and our pastor was talking about going to Haiti. During church, Andy and I looked at each other and said, "She's going to go to Haiti, isn't she?" On the way home in the car, "Mom, can I go to Haiti?" We said, "Yes" without much hesitation.

> *The heart of man plans his way,*
> *but the Lord establishes his steps.*
> PROVERBS 16:9

We knew the plan was to help Lucy experience other cultures. Now God was laying out the steps. For whatever reason, God needed Lucy to see extreme poverty. That was part of her trajectory.

But the steps were up to God. We didn't get on the computer and immediately show her photos and videos of poverty and starvation. We waited for God to determine those steps. And that first step was Haiti.

3. Release the Arrow
Let go and trust.

When I first was writing this, I thought my "release the arrow" example with Lucy would be when we let her go to Burkina Faso with a group we didn't know too much about. But deep in my heart, I could hear something saying, "Janet, that's not when you released that arrow." And I knew. With Lucy's permission, I share when we experienced the greatest season of letting her go.

Story Time:

Lucy has always been the type of person to ask questions. She never really wanted to accept things just because someone said she should. That part of her became much louder her senior year of high school. Her questions became more frequent. She started making choices that pushed our boundaries. I remember one conversation in particular where she said (through many tears), "But if God doesn't exist, none of this even matters." Andy and I felt like a stake had been driven through our hearts. We were so tempted to go after her with all of our knowledge and scripture and experience, and when she asked, we did do that. But I'll tell you most of our time was spent praying things like this:

God, she's Your daughter. You made her. Thank You for letting us partner with You in raising her. And now, we let her go.

You are her perfect Parent. We're not.

You love her perfectly. We don't.

You see what's truly in her heart. We can't.

We open our hands and ask You to take her. Move in and through her.

We are choosing to let go. We choose to trust You.

These prayers were prayed through many, many tears and a lot of fear. We desperately wanted to fix everything, but we knew God was urging us to let go and trust Him. So we kept the lines of communication and connection open with her as much as we could and chose to believe that God loves her even more than we do.

> *Trust in the Lord with all your heart,*
>   *and do not lean on your own understanding.*
> *In all your ways acknowledge him,*
>   *and he will make straight your paths.*
> PROVERBS 3:5-6

Lucy has landed on Jesus. She's still working out some of those questions but she trusts us and she's learning from the Holy Spirit and the Word, not just from other people. If she continues to travel to other countries, she will need those skills more than she'll need anything else. Our letting go enabled her to be strengthened.

So, what do we do with all of this? Here's a good starting point:

Take time to listen to God about your kids.

I remember a few years ago I was at a parenting workshop. My friend, Dree was speaking and she gave us time to listen to what God has to say about our kids. The one that stands out to me the most is what God told me about Eve, our youngest daughter. He told me that Eve needs to know she's a seed, not a stone. And that's something we still pray over her. She is a life-giver, not a stone.

As I said in chapter 3, our children, when launched out into the world, are meant to do damage to the kingdom of darkness.

What does God see in your child?

Let's go over that list from chapter 3 again.

Does God see your child as

    A lie buster?

    A darkness illuminator?

    A confusion clarifier?

    A truth speaker?

    A freedom fighter?

Write it down and talk about it with your spouse, a mentor or parent.

Ask God this question, "Do I speak this to my child or tuck this away in prayer?"

It's time to set, aim and release those arrows.

Moving Forward

by Janet Mylin

I go through life like a boxer beating the air.

Like a person who's just walked through a
spider web.

Like a toddler trying to catch a bubble.

Like a gregarious woman explaining a story with
her hands.

Like a dog chasing after its own tail.

I go through life like a dog returning to its vomit.

Like a drunk and the bar.

Like a dog and Easter chocolate.

Like a cat and toxic houseplants.

Like a woman and fashion magazines.

I go through life running aimlessly.

Like a stink bug in flight.

Like a june bug on the end of a string.

Like a leaf in the wind.

Like trash in the ocean.

I go through life.

I want life to go through me.

Like a river through a valley.

Like icing through a pastry bag.

Like a racehorse through the starting gate.

Like eyesight through lenses.

PART THREE

The
Terrible

CHAPTER 8
What's Terrible?

Why would I call this section The Terrible?

Because we can't continue working towards our true identity as women who operate in the role of "mother" without addressing some of the pain surrounding it.

The truth is, when I say the word "mom", some of you are filled with warm feelings and some of you are filled with negative feelings...or maybe filled with a sense of emptiness. (Isn't it strange how *emptiness* can actually *fill* you?)

> Compliments about who you are as a mom Do. Not. Land.
>
> Mother's Day is filled with angst.
>
> Affectionate mothers and daughters make you roll your eyes, assuming it's fake.
>
> Commercials, TV shows, and movies portraying connective moms make your eyes fill with tears of "I wish..."

Frankly, for some, the word "mother" is the same as saying the worst swear word you know.

The pain you have surrounding that word is insurmountable and suffocating - especially if you've endured trauma as a result of your mother's action or inaction.

And now here you are.

Either you are a mom or you intend to become one.

How in the world do you thrive in that role when you're drawing from an empty well?

Is it even possible???

Take a minute and write down or draw what the word "mother" means for you.

I suppose I could list all the ways a woman can end up with a broken view of motherhood, but I'm not convinced that's the best approach. It might just cause us to compare our pain or experience, and that's no good. Suffice it to say, all of our mothers are broken in some way. And some mothers' brokenness has caused huge gaping wounds in our lives - whether intentional or not. What matters now is what we do with that pain.

CHAPTER 9
The Well

I want to begin this section on The Terrible with a word picture. I have a dear friend. A woman of the Word. A woman who pursues freedom with intensity. I learn so much from her. As she was working through her own mother wounds, the Spirit gave her a very clear picture of what she was doing every time she went to her mother as her source of security, instead of to God.

This writing is raw. Her relationship with her mother is depicted as a dry well and the allegory could easily be applied to any relationship. The Lord is depicted as a lush waterfall. I pray and trust the Holy Spirit will walk you through this as you feel empathy, loss, encouragement or conviction. Find a quiet place to sit and read this. Actually, I would recommend you read it out loud. At my friend's request, we'll respect her anonymity.

The Well

God, I can see me waiting by an almost empty well for any kind of condensation to come from it.

I can see You - You the vast waterfall, off in a lush forest, teeming with life.

Me, over by the well, cursing You for not loving me.

Blistered by the sun, angry at the empty well.

My days feel consumed with watching others drink deeply of the falls, splash and dive and also me staring at the dry well, willing You to come and smite it.

I hear myself tell You that once You destroy this barren well, I'll come drink deep, too.

The well still stands.

My heart breaks.

"Why do You have to hurt me like this??"

"Why can't You love me??" Looking at both the well and the falls that time.

I scream and curse and cry at You, then the well,

back at You, then at some passers by, then back to the well.

In the panic of my heat stroke, I don't know who I want to hate more.

I can't decide.

I create mirages - I KNOW they're fake, but I long, so painfully, to see them. To pretend it's in my reach.

I sit by the well.

My back against the hard brick.

Sun beating down on my head and body.

I stare off longingly at my sweet mirages.

I can almost feel water on my tongue when I look at my smoke screen of oases.

I don't want to leave.

But it fuels my anger instead of subsiding it.

It fans my hate instead of giving me love.

Even these mirages have failed me, too.

I lie there, listless, hopeless, depressed.

Both unable to leave this dry well and unable to drink from a mirage.

I hear the waters calling me - I hear the roar of the falls, but my heart is so hard.

Then my deepest fear comes into the light: What if THAT is just a mirage too?

What if the sound of water- the lush green and the cool breeze is something I can get close to, but not touch?

What if I can never get past the brim of it - what if I can only smell the mist in the air and try to drink it like a shameless beast, but never feel the cool on my tongue or the shade over my rigid body?

What if my worst fear is realized and I find myself running ravenously from one mirage to another.... Unceasingly.

I don't know how to get there!!! Can't You see that??!

What if You're not there?
Or I'm not allowed there?

I'm already here.

Come with Me.

My body bore the sun's heat, so you could sit in the shade of My arms.

The fire bore into My back so you'd never be alone at the dry well.

I was always here.

My back against the same rough brick.

Whispering to you, telling you how much I loved you and inviting you into the garden - while you were looking for the water at this well.

I never condemned you or shamed you for not hearing My voice and I never will. I only tell you now because I want you to know.

I drink this cup He offered.

I drank the cup empty, but there was more.

He kept whispering, *"It's ok. You're ok."*

Up against His chest and the mere scent of Him becomes aloe to the blisters that cover me.

I breathe in the scent heavily.

"Drink again. I never want you to thirst."

Then it hits me - I'm the woman at the well - who can't stop going to my broken cisterns, so I have to go to the well in the heat of the day.

He was there.

At the well, He was there!

I'd never seen Him there before, but He was.

He sat in the heat with me.

For me.

I've cursed those on their way to the falls and I cursed the ones already there.

You've sat by the angry girl at the dry well.... Why did You do that??

My best days were when I thought I heard You speak to me, and now I know it was *really You*.

I'm a beggar

An orphan

A harlot

Determined to wrangle love out of whoever I can just to prove that I'm lovable.

And still You sat by *me*.

I feel the bounce in His step as He carries me away from the dry well and towards the falls.

I'm still scared it might not be real, but He's not afraid of or offended by my fear. He keeps carrying me away from the empty well.

We're not to the falls yet, but I I hope we get there soon.

Do you have a dried-up well relationship in your life?

Describe how you could relate to this allegory.

How does it go for you when you continually go to an unhealthy relationship as a source of security?

What is one practical thing you can do today to keep you from being drawn back to that empty well?

Have you had "lush waterfall" experiences - times when you've felt closer to the Lord than ever before?

What was that time like?

CHAPTER 10
The Rage Train

Jack was little. Like "using a purple plastic step stool to reach the bathroom sink" little. It was time to wash his hands. He put his tiny fingers into the stream of water. I calmly said, "Jack you need to wash all of your hands, not just the fingers." He put his hands in a little bit more, but still not the whole hand. In a stroke of genius, I instructed, "When you wash your hands, you need to get your wrists wet." He looked at me and stuck his hands a little deeper into the water. I said it *again* in a more punctuated tone, "Jack. Get. Your. Wrists. Wet. *NOW*."

Jack refused to obey.

You've been there, right? What starts as a simple lesson in washing your hands, turns into an epic battle. Each time I urged my son to get his wrists wet, more and more fire grew beneath it.

Then it happened.

The wheels came off.

The proverbial poop hit the fan.

Like a 13 year old girl at a boy band concert, *I lost my ever-loving mind*.

I screamed with a voice from the very bowels of Hell, *"GET YOUR WRISTS WET!!!"* I screamed so hard and loud I actually had to bend over to get the words out.

Jack started crying. (Of course, he did. He thought his mom was Satan.)

I grabbed him, way too harshly.

Taking him to his room, I sat him down in his chair, way too hard, stormed out of his room and slammed the door behind me loudly.

As I stood on the other side of that door, breathing hard and trying to come down from the high that comes with the release of rage, God interrupted my thoughts abruptly and clearly:

"Janet, he doesn't know what a wrist is."

Instantly, all of the anger blew out of me like helium from a balloon.

Yikes. *Double and triple yikes*.

I opened Jack's door and walked over to the little whimpering boy in the chair.

"Jack, do you know what a wrist is?"

With quivering lips, he said, "No!!"

Sobs. Big sobs. From both of us.

In my imagination, sometimes I picture Anger as a disillusioned lump of coal. And, since this is *my* imagination, it has eyes.

To me, my anger is like a lump of coal that is trying to create diamonds. It uses outbursts and rage as a way of creating enough pressure and heat to hopefully force whoever is in front of me into beauty, strength, and perfection.

FYI, that's how diamonds are made. With heat and pressure. But did you know diamonds are not actually made from lumps of coal? It's true they are both made from carbon, but coal has too many impurities to actually become the wonder that is a diamond.

Yes, you can buy lab-created diamonds. But their worth pales in comparison to a diamond that has been created by God in the secret place with just enough pressure and just the right amount of heat. A diamond created by God is a hidden miracle, until it is discovered.

That's what I see Anger trying to do: Create enough heat and pressure to turn my kids into diamonds. Beautiful, strong, perfect. Something that makes my life easier.

But it is a futile effort. Anger can't do that. Only God can truly create that kind of beauty and strength.

I saw a movie where a witch put a curse on a young girl, only to regret it later. When she spoke the curse, she was full of anger and jealousy. But her heart changed and she realized it was a mistake. There's a compelling scene when the witch is desperately trying to revoke the curse as the young girl sleeps. But she can't.

The curse had landed and could not be revoked.

I wept during that scene. I could never count all the times I've felt the same way...desperately hoping my angry words and actions don't take root in my child's life. "Please, God. Have mercy on me. Have mercy on my child. Will you please wipe away the sin of this day? Can you please help my child just forget this day ever happened?" Have you felt that way?

Take a minute to write about how all of that makes you feel right now in this moment.

A friend was telling me of a day she had. It was "one of those days." Emotions were running high, things kept escalating until finally, she lost it. She had boarded the rage train and she was taking all three kids with her. The whole day was wrought with yelling and crying.

But let me tell what she did at the end of that really hard day.

She crawled into bed beside the child that had borne the main brunt of the anger and she apologized. She talked about confession and God's forgiveness. She extended grace to her daughter. She extended grace to herself. She invited her daughter to do the same. And they both basked in the grace of God.

That is everything.

One time one of our children confessed a hard thing to us. It wasn't the worst thing in the world. The child didn't start a cult and force hundreds of people to drink poison kool-aid. But it was a thing that made our knees shake. When my husband and I went for a walk to process this together, I had one very clear reality in front of me: **This child's sinful choices were not mine to own. But the fact that my precious child came to me and trusted me enough to get vulnerable and confess IS mine to own.** That is on me. That right there is the fruit from years of crawling into bed with my kids after I've taken them for a ride on my Rage Train and humbling myself, confessing and talking about God's forgiveness.

I can't own or control my kids' sinful choices, but I *can* own their ability to come to me and trust me with their brokenness.

Some of our actions will add impurities to those circumstances and memories, but we need to trust God will create beauty out of it in the secret places of life, trial, and faith.

If your kids are perfected immediately, where is their story? The heat and pressure of life do indeed naturally happen under God's loving care. And He will lead them towards maturity, healing, and wholeness. Your anger and controlling behavior is not going to hurry the maturing process along.

When are you most tempted to give into rage, hoping it will change your child's behavior?

Write it down. No guilt if you feel that way all of the time.

Some things that have helped me along the way in dealing with rage:

• Control something other than your child. Something that can't be affected by your negative emotions. An inanimate object. (Furniture, cleaning, haircut, punching bag, etc.)

• Say to yourself, "My anger can only change his actions, not his heart. Only God can change a heart."

• Whisper, don't yell.

• If you tend to disconnect and go silent when you're angry as a way to manipulate your child, make yourself look them in the eyes for 30 seconds or force yourself to stay in the same room as your child. Don't leave them unless you know you're going to hurt them by staying.

• Take a second alone in the bathroom, closet, car, or wherever and ask yourself, "What am I *actually* mad about?" Oftentimes, it's not the child. Your child and your ability to influence them may just be the most convenient outlet for your rage.

CHAPTER 11
Two Ugly Words

Throughout the course of life, we brush up against two things that can have incredible influence in how we act and react to our children.

Sin and Trauma.

In my experience, when I courageously choose to face the consequences of sin and trauma head-on instead of ignoring or running away from them, I grow deep roots in my faith.

The thing is when trauma is done to me, it can easily become sin against someone else. And that is the cycle we want...*need* to break in our families.

When you look at your life, either in the past or currently, do the people who have hurt you the most have unhealed trauma in their life? Mine do. And even if I don't know what the trauma was, I can see it there. You can see it in others, can't you? Can you see it in yourself?

Here's some space for rumination, if you feel the need.

It seems impossible, or maybe less fruitful, to talk about motherhood without addressing the "terrible" that comes along with the sin and trauma in our lives. In fact, I would go as far as to say that it's difficult to talk about growing in *any* area of our lives without addressing sin and trauma. The most fruitful seasons of deep, lasting change in my life have come from looking pain and sin square in the eyes and saying, "I am determined to heal from this, and I am determined to grow from it!"

The actual practical steps of healing from sin and trauma can vary for individuals, but my own healing has come through:

Professional counseling

Peer counseling

Mentoring

Truth-filled books

Exercise

Eating healthy food

Rest

Truth prayer (essentially identifying lies and replacing them with truth, as you ask the Lord to uproot and cut off anything that hinders you)

Scripture reading and meditation

Worship, worship and WORSHIP

Gratitude for what God has done and is doing

Transparency in safe community

Sleep medication for different seasons

And probably many other things here and there.

The main thing is, once you've identified an area of sin or trauma that needs healing, go after it.

Like a kid chasing an ice cream truck.

Like a dog going after his favorite squeaky toy.

Like a mama bear protecting her cubs.

Like a flower reaching for the sunlight.

Do not let anything deter you.

I like how The Passion Translation puts it.

> *Let me be clear, the Anointed One has set us free—not partially, but completely and wonderfully free! We must always cherish this truth and stubbornly refuse to go back into the bondage of our past.*
> GALATIANS 5:1

But I need to be straight up with you about something. The journey towards freedom from sin and trauma is life-changing, but it isn't necessarily smooth. As you get closer to the pain, you might get frantic and want to just run from it.

Don't. *You just can't.*

Stay the course. Don't give up. Keep doing the things that move you towards wholeness. God is moving. None of your story will be wasted.

A Dare

by Janet Mylin

How dare the snow fall wherever it wants.

How dare that purity would fall upon the dirt – making it beautiful.

How dare that snow fall and remind me of who I am.

Feel like writing a poem? Go ahead. There are no rules. Just start.

PART FOUR

The
Crown

CHAPTER 12
Prostitutes and Kings

When I first began asking the Holy Spirit to teach me about motherhood and what it really means to be a "good mom," I was taken to a very unusual story. Honestly, I was kind of relieved because I was truly afraid the Spirit was going to be like, "Just memorize and do Proverbs 31." Not that Proverbs 31 isn't a fine example of motherhood, wife-hood (Wife-dom? Wife-ness?), womanhood, and many other things. She is all of those things. However, I needed a fresh perspective. I was so asleep in my view of motherhood that "Charm is deceitful and beauty is vain..." wasn't going to be enough initially to wake me up.

The Spirit's lesson plan began with a very unlikely teacher. A prostitute. Well, actually two prostitutes. If you're into it, you can read the story in 1 Kings 3:16-28. It's just 12 verses long. For those of you who just want to stay right here, I'll outline the story for you. For the sake of clarity, let's call them Woman 1 and Woman 2.

1. King Solomon is the wisest and wealthiest king in the world (1 Kings 10:23).

2. Two prostitutes, Woman 1 and Woman 2, who lived in the same house, came to him one day with a baby.

3. Woman 1 told Solomon that she had given birth to a child. She said Woman 2 gave birth to a baby three days after her but rolled on her baby in the night, thus accidentally killing the baby. Woman 1 went on to say Woman 2 took her baby in the middle of the night and replaced that baby with her own lifeless child. But when Woman 1 woke up and carefully looked at the baby in her bed, she realized it wasn't the baby she had borne.

4. Woman 2 said, "No. That's not right. The dead child is yours and the living child is mine."

5. King Solomon stated the obvious problem, "Well, you're both telling me the living baby is yours."

6. King Solomon told someone to bring him a sword. He proclaimed the plan in verse 25: "Divide the living child in two. Give half to Woman 1 and half to Woman 2."

7. Woman 1 immediately begged the King to give the living baby to the other woman so the baby would not be put to death.

8. Woman 2 agreed with the king's plan, basically saying, "He's not going to belong to either of us. Divide the baby in half."

9. Right away Solomon was able to identify the baby's mother. In verse 27 he said, "Give the living child to the first woman, and by no means put him to death; she is his mother."

Fascinating, right? The first time I read that story, I was like, "Solomon was a GENIUS!" And apparently everyone else who heard about it thought the same because they were even more nuts over Solomon's wisdom thereafter.

The following chapters will break down some mini-teachings on what these two women taught me about motherhood.

CHAPTER 13
Accept Our Weaknesses

We need to accept the fact that our own shortcomings and mistakes are going to have some sort of negative impact on our children - some have greater impact than others.

We have no reason to believe the smothering of the woman's baby was intentional. It appears as though she was sleeping with her baby and accidentally, tragically rolled onto him. We can assume she woke up and, to her horror, realized what happened.

Can you even *imagine*?

Some of you can. Unbearable, crushing pain.

And no matter how accidental it was...no matter how many times she ran it over in her mind...it seems like one question would pound against her already pounding heart, "What if..."

> *What if I had put a better barrier between us?*
> *What if I wouldn't have run myself into the ground*

with exhaustion so I would have woken up?
What if...
What if...
What if...

Unresolved "what ifs" can be open doors to unbearable guilt.

Regardless of whether or not you can relate to Woman 2's actual story, I wonder: How many times have you looked at your child's face, knowing your weaknesses and humanness have extracted a little air out of her lungs?

For me? Too many to count. And the guilt has, at times, been paralyzing.

I am learning my weaknesses are actually part of my child's story. Hear me: That doesn't give me a license to be abusive, thinking, "Well, God will redeem this so I'm gonna unleash all of my rage, angst and wounds on my children." As Paul said in Romans 6:1-2, "What shall we say then? Are we to continue in sin that grace may abound? By no means! How can we who died to sin still live in it?" Knowing God will bring redemption for our children doesn't mean we can do whatever we want, depending on God's grace to make it all better somewhere down the road.

However, there's a beautiful scripture that should be like an anchor for moms (and well, any human).

> *But he (the Lord) said to me, "My grace is sufficient for you, for my power is made perfect in weakness." Therefore I will boast all the more gladly of my weaknesses, so that the power of Christ may rest upon me. For the sake of Christ, then, I am content with weaknesses, insults, hardships, persecutions, and calamities. For when I am weak, then I am strong.*
> 2 CORINTHIANS 12:9-10

You see, Paul had a "thorn in his side." From what I can tell, no one really knows what the thorn was...a medical problem, a relational issue, insomnia, possibly an eye problem...we don't know. But from what I can tell, it was way more intense than, "I get gassy when I eat hummus."

Verse 8 says he asked the Lord three times to remove this "thorn" and God's message was clear: Our weaknesses are like a magnifying glass on God's strength.

Going back to our grieving prostitute friend and the tragic loss of her baby, we can ask a different What If:

> What if we could get to a place where we quickly land on God's ability to make something beautiful out of any situation - no matter how hopeless it appears to be? What if hope became our knee-jerk reaction to every situation in which our weakness hurts our kids?

What was your initial reaction to Woman 2 when you first heard the story?

Did you feel empathy, disdain or a little bit of both?

Now that we've talked about her a little more, have your feelings towards Woman 2 changed? Why or why not?

It is impossible to live life without struggle. The very fact that we are mothers is a promise that we will experience heartache of all depths through our children's experiences. The key is to press into God's grace for us, instead of trying to fix everything.

Now let's talk about control.

CHAPTER 14
Hyper-Control

Hyper-control is never the answer.

Even though this story is not likely to be something we've experienced exactly, we can relate to Woman 2's reaction. Don't we all know what it's like to feel entirely out of control of a situation?

I remember sitting on the plane on our way to China to pick up Eve, our daughter. I vacillated wildly between "I'm so excited to have another daughter!" and "What if she hates me? What if she's horrible?" We had done everything we could to find out as much about her as possible before bringing her into our family, but ultimately, it was really out of our hands. Eve had 9 years of experiences under her belt of which I was largely ignorant. And that was scary.

Eventually, we have to land on faith in God's love for us.

Frantic controlling is never a place of peace.

Have you ever seen a movie where chaos is happening and there's one person who's running around like a maniac, screaming and doing dumb things in their panic? Oftentimes, someone with a level head will go to that wild person and *SLAP* right across the face. Why? To bring them back to a useful place in reality. To get them to "snap out of it." To remind them that, even in the midst of utter chaos, they can make life-giving choices.

The grieving woman in our story was in such a frantic state and rightfully so. The intense, physiological longing to hold a baby in her arms compelled her to take another child - bringing tragedy to another woman in order to fabricate peace for herself. If only someone could have gotten a hold of her saying, "You have every right to feel all of your feelings. This is an awful tragedy. The pain you feel is real. But taking matters into your own hands and replacing your baby with a stolen child is not the answer. Let's walk through this together."

Has anyone ever gotten you to calm down in the midst of a chaotic season of life?

What did they do? How did you respond?

What is the last thing you frantically tried to control in the midst of feeling out of control in some area of your life?

Did your mom, dad, or authority figure ever act out in hyper-controlling you?

Ask the Holy Spirit to remove that control connection from your life so you can walk in freedom.

CHAPTER 15

Break the Crown

It's an identity issue.

All through these lessons, have you been thinking, "Well, they're prostitutes. What do I have in common with them, really?" I get that. While some of you may have prostitution as part of your story, the odds are, most of you don't.

But here's the thing: you're still broken. You're still probably "prone to wander." So let's not get into a finger-pointing mode over the vocation of these two women and what we may or may not think they deserve. Instead, let's view them as women who, for whatever reasons, landed in a very broken place.

Okay, now that we agree about that, let's go into this a little more deeply.

We have one woman who was so determined to be known as a mom, that she committed a terrible crime in order to make that happen.

Why was this so important to her?

> Maybe she felt proving herself as a mom would be her way out of the sex trade industry.

> Maybe she was deeply craving real human connection and holding her baby met that need.

> Maybe, when she looked into her baby's eyes, she saw a sense of purpose for the first time ever in her life.

> Maybe it was for less noble reasons.

Regardless, she was entirely focused on maintaining her role as Mother.

And then we have Woman 1. As far as we can tell, her life's circumstances are pretty much the same as her housemate. She likely fell in love when she first counted her newborn babe's fingers and toes. She probably felt overwhelmed at the questions and responsibility that comes with having a baby. Lots of normal feelings. And, when Solomon makes the grotesque suggestion of cutting the baby in half, she is the first to choose saving the baby's life, even though it meant another woman would be raising him.

Let's combine our imaginations with the Holy Spirit for a minute here. Woman 1 knew if King Solomon gave the baby to the other woman, she would be watching someone else raise her child *in the same house*. It wasn't like Woman 2 would take her baby and move to another city or country. This lying woman was going to be mothering her child *right in front of her eyes*, day in and day out. Can you begin to imagine the pain? I can't.

But, to her, the baby's chance at life was greater than her desire to cling to the physical role of Mother.

As circumstances would have it, I'm currently sitting at a table in our mall typing this out. A woman is carrying a newborn baby past me and the baby is crying. (You know, that little cry where they don't even really quite sound human yet?) And I'm imagining myself as the woman from our Bible story, laying in my bed at night, hearing *my newborn child* crying in the other room, unable to do anything about it. Sobbing and wailing into my pillow, feeling my milk let down, looking for a place of release. The agony would have been unbearable. But she was willing to walk through it for the sake of her child's life, even if it meant no one ever knew she had a child. Even if no one would ever tell her she's a good mom. Even if her child grew up to know her as just a woman who lived in their house.

I do realize there is a chance she felt unworthy to mother a child, just like many of us. But, even so, she did not seem to look at that infant and say, "You are the one who will make me feel better about myself. You have the power to change my identity so I will frantically and fearfully hold onto you, no matter what."

There is a Really Big Question looming in the air. Do you feel it, too?

Is your whole identity wrapped up in your role as a Mother?

Or is your identity in God, your Creator, your King, your perfect adoptive Father?

Write your thoughts here.

Do you feel the weight of being the source of identity for your parents?

Why do you think that is?

Do these two women actually represent every mom's struggle?

One woman's decisions beg the question: "What are we willing to break in our children in order to make ourselves appear or feel whole?"

The other woman's decisions ask: "What are we willing to have broken in our own lives in order to preserve our children's wholeness?

She was willing to lay down her chance at receiving a "Mother of the Year" crown for the sake of choosing wholeness and life for her child.

What does her decision remind us to do? **Break the crown, not the arrow.**

CHAPTER 16
Mending the Arrows

The truth is, we will wound our children.
Isn't it unavoidable?

Whenever you have two imperfect humans rubbing shoulders regularly, you will hurt each other. And when one of those humans is in a position of authority over the other, the door is wide open for hurts, misunderstandings and dysfunctional patterns.

The beautiful thing is this:

> We get to help our children heal from wounds - even if we're the ones who did the wounding. This may be a hands-on experience or it may be through the power of prayer.

When my oldest was little, I inadvertently put the label of "Inconvenient" on her. Now I know kids' needs and wants are largely not convenient. There's some truth in that. But my actions (and sometimes my words) reemphasized to her over and over "Your needs are always in the way of my desires."

As she grew, I could see the effects of that label fleshing out in her life. Some of it is her personality, but I would cringe with a dose of shame as I watched her not want to inconvenience people, or ask for help, or use her voice. When she was old enough to understand, I began talking to her about how I was part of the reason she felt that way. Yes, I even apologized for it, although she was probably too young to understand the weight of it.

And thus began a journey of me walking my daughter through healing from this label I helped to create.

I know, right? Feels a little hypocritical, doesn't it?

It also feels like a truckload of grace. More grace than I deserve, for sure. And a huge dose of humility. Humility I didn't think I had.

This is another glimpse of how motherhood is a dim reflection of the nurturing acts of the Holy Spirit.

Just as the Holy Spirit came to remind us of Truth (John 14:26), when we see lies producing "fruit" in the lives of our sons and daughters, we need to remind them of the Truth that combats those lies - no matter where the lies originated.

Can you imagine if someone who wounded you humbly came alongside you to help you move on and thrive as you heal from those wounds? Can you imagine if that person was your mother or father? *Powerful.*

We can partner with the Holy Spirit in our kids' healing through intercession, truth-speaking and a humble listening ear.

Even if, for various reasons, we can't physically, tangibly come alongside them, we can commit their healing to the Lord in prayer.

Think back to Woman 1. (Again, you can read the story in the Bible at 1 Kings 3:16-28.) In my mind, when I try to jump into her thoughts after she tells Solomon to give the baby to the other woman, this is how it goes:

> *"All my toxic choices have culminated in this moment. I must deserve this. I have this tiny, defenseless baby and now he'll be raised by a liar. But maybe..just maybe...I'll be able to come*

alongside him in some way as he lives in our house. Maybe I'll be able to tell him how great he is as I pass him in the hallway. Maybe I can slip him healthy food once in a while if she doesn't provide it for him. Maybe she'll even let me take care of him sometimes when she is weary of him. And maybe, just maybe, God will listen to me if I ask Him to take care of my son. Maybe God will hold him when I can't. Maybe God will hold me, too. Maybe we can both heal from these unbearable wounds."

For many of you, a mother who humbly owns up to her sin *and* equips her kids to walk in God's Truth will change the definition of "motherhood" in your lineage for generations to come. Is that generation-changing mom *you*?

What do you think about owning up to it when you sin against your kids?

How do you honestly feel about God being more present and powerful in your kids' lives than you are?

Do you know someone who has a "walk alongside them in their pain" sort of relationship with their older child? If you're compelled, give them a call and ask how they've cultivated such a relationship.

A word on over-apologizing:

Matthew 5:33-37 talks about the importance of being a person of your word. It's speaking specifically about making vows, but I always remember it when it comes to lots of other things, too. When I apologize to someone and they extend forgiveness, I do my best to leave it and not grovel or keep asking for forgiveness.

We are modeling repentance and forgiveness to our kids. If we constantly follow them around asking them to forgive us and whining about how messed up we are, our apologies will lose weight. But if we intentionally apologize for a specific sin against them, accept their forgiveness and move on, they will understand the gravity of that act of humility and the power of extending and receiving forgiveness.

How do you decide when an apology is necessary? Ask the Holy Spirit.

Have trouble trusting the Holy Spirit? You're going to really dig chapter 21.

CHAPTER 17
Super Mother

Not too long ago, our Sunday morning church service was disrupted by a desperate woman in the throes of a crisis. I and others immediately went into action in different ways...holding her, staying with her, initiating prayer, communicating the necessities. It was the Body of Christ in action.

It wasn't until the end of that very hard day when I saw something remarkable. My friend sent me a text. He was encouraging me and talking about the experience from his point of view. He recounted every person he saw do different things in the midst of the crisis moment. He said the names of different people who moved and lead. *All of them were mothers.*

He said, "No one other than mothers grabbed the reins and led today."

And as if someone had turned on a light bulb in a dark room, I saw the day with greater clarity.

No one could just start hugging hurting people like a mother.

No one can see a need for snacks, drinks, and

other physical needs as quickly as a mother.

No one can sit and listen quite like a mother.

No one can immediately cry tears of empathy quite like a mother.

No one can immediately love another's child like her own, if the need arises, like a mother can.

And these words came out of my mouth: Motherhood is exactly and truly a super-power.

It is a gift given by our Divine Creator - whether we have children or not. **Women are supernaturally empowered to mother.**

Nurture.

Care.

Meet needs.

Solve problems.

Help the hurting.

Get to work.

Roll up our sleeves.

If you need something done, you ask a mother, and if she can't do it, she'll find someone who can. We should not bemoan the fact that we are mothers (even though raising children is *just so hard*). Nor should we bemoan the fact that men often aren't naturally endowed with the same abilities. Motherhood is a gift, and it is needed literally everywhere. No human is without the need of mothering.

(And, yes, I feel the same way about fatherhood.)

When I see it this way, it removes the temptation to compare myself to other moms. I can look at a mom who makes color-coded charts and think, "That's awesome! That's a gift for her kids!" I can see the woman who has six-pack abs and gets her kids outside every day and I can cheer her on! The woman who only feeds her kids organic food can get me excited because I know she's nurturing her kids in exactly the way she feels is best for them! And hopefully other women can look at me - a mom who takes naps, goes to bed with dirty dishes in the sink and has occasional dance parties with her kids - and they can say "I'm just so glad you are in the world!"

In Luke 13:34, it speaks of the Lord wanting to gather Jerusalem's children "...as a hen gathers her brood under her wings..." Could anything sound more motherly than that?

Is there a time when you could see that God was gathering you under His wings like a hen gathers her chicks?

How did that feel? Did you know it was happening in real time, or did you not really see it that way until later on?

Silencing the Voices

by Janet Mylin

What is a great mom?

Everything? Is she everything?
Oh God, I hope not.

Nothing? Is she nothing?
Dear God, say it isn't so.

Perfect? Is she perfect?
Good Lord, that can't be.

Controlling? Is she controlling?
King of Everything, that's exhausting.

Humble? Is she humble?
Abba, that's probably true.

Kind? Is she kind?
Abba, that rings clear in my mind.

Wise? Is she wise?
Abba, you provide that.

Connected? Is she connected?
Abba, that's what you do.

Joy-filled? Is she joy-filled?
Abba, that sounds like freedom.

PART FIVE

The Invitation

CHAPTER 18
Candy Superstitions

Do you remember how in at the end of Chapter Two, I said we'd work through your own broken views of the Holy Spirit? Well, here we are. Why are we doing this? Because I found I couldn't operate as a whole, loving, powerful, nurturing mother until I saw the perfect nature of the ever-present Holy Spirit more clearly.

Have you heard about being "filled with the Holy Spirit" or "living the Spirit-filled life"? What honest thoughts, memories and feelings do these phrases bring out in you?

Write them down here, even if they feel really wrong or unbiblical.

Before we talk about asking for more of the Holy Spirit, let me share some of my own story with you.

I gave my life to Jesus when I was in 7th grade at a youth group event in Lancaster, PA. I immediately crashed and burned into a middle-school-level oblivion of sin, shame and doing my own thing. I rededicated my life to Him a year or so later. What can I say? I was complicated.

I had times when I felt like God directed me or spoke to me in kind of obscure ways. I believed He spoke. But it wasn't until I joined a missions organization right out of high school that I was actually taught how to hear God's voice. It was so cool! I had never just quieted myself to "listen" to what God put into my thoughts before that time and I was *all in*. It brought a whole new level of intimacy into my young prayer life.

I remember a tender season of asking God who on the Earth needs prayer and sometimes I would get a clear picture of a human I had never seen before in my mind. I would launch into praying for him or her as if they were sitting right in front of me. It was powerful! I really believed I was partnering with God to influence someone I'd never met, and likely would never meet on Earth.

In the midst of this season I began dating a boy (not my husband). He had grown up differently than I. He was full of a spiritual boldness I'd never seen in a guy my age before. I fell hook, line, and sinker for him. Honestly, falling hook, line and sinker for boys came very easily to me. But that's another book.

Our relationship morphed into a sort of dysfunctional mentoring situation where he told me how the Holy Spirit worked, I believed it completely, and desperately tried to live it. Looking back, we were just two kids with a lot of zeal and not a lot of maturity.

As a result of that relationship and a few other things going on in my world at that time, I came to believe some untruths about myself and the Lord, but the one that was most overwhelming was this:

I need a "direct word from the Spirit" to make any decision, large or small.

Did anyone specifically tell me that? No. I don't believe so. But that is how my 19 year old mind interpreted the actions and words of those around me.

Oh. And I should mention one important piece of this story. We were serving overseas during this season of dating. And since it was the early 90's, I had no email, Internet, or easy phone access at that point to bounce things off my parents or mentors back home.

This began a painful season of transformation for me. I transformed from "Confident Fun-Loving Christian Girl" to "Insecure Frantic Hoping She's Okay Girl." I became completely superstitious with my faith because I was frantic about hearing God's voice. Terrified someone would prophesy over me and expose how much of a Christian I *wasn't*. Positive my leaders and boyfriend were talking behind my back about the hopeless state of Janet.

What did this look like for me on a daily basis?

Praying over a Snickers bar.

For real. I was living in a formerly Communist nation about a year after Communism fell and certain Western comforts were not easily accessible at that point. Specifically, I'm talking about Snickers bars. They were like the Golden Ticket on Willy Wonka. That doesn't mean they were necessarily expensive; it means they were hard to find.

When I would spot one of those delightful bars of goodness from my homeland, I could not - would not - just pick it up and buy it. I would pray about it. It would look something like this:

> *"Lord, should I buy this Snickers bar? I have the money to buy it. I don't need the money for anything else. But what if...I buy it and then I meet someone who needed that money? What if you actually need me to spend that $1 on something else? Would I be sinning to buy this Snickers bar? Or maybe You need me to buy two of them? Is that what you want? Do you need me to buy one for me and one for someone else? Is that Your holy purpose for the $1 in my hand? Oh, God! I don't want to miss Your will for me in this moment! What should I do?"*

All the while, I felt this was how holy people lived. I thought that was the Holy Spirit's purpose. To micro-manage every detail of my life and if I missed it, I was sunk. Or at the very least, way less blessed than all the other hyper-spiritual people around me who appeared to be nailing it every time.

How did this translate when I got home?

Me at a four-way stop sign, having a panic attack

because what if I went the "wrong" way and missed something huge God had for me?

Me buying gum at the checkout and changing my mind many times until I found the gum I felt God really wanted me to buy.

Some of you might be like, *"You've GOT to be kidding me!"* - especially if you know me now - as a whole, healed, Spirit-filled woman.

And yet, others of you. Something about this resonates hard with you. Like me, you cringe a little when you read it.

If that's you, write about that here. Just a few sentences to express what you're feeling right now:

CHAPTER 19
Look at You

So the big question is: How did I move on from this? Where did I find healing in my view of the Holy Spirit's role in my life? You read about part of that healing in chapter 2. Let me share two steps that helped me.

Step 1: I had to be willing to see myself differently than what I was used to.

After I got back to the States, the people who had known me most of my life treated me like they saw something in me I couldn't see. Whether it was as a youth group leader or as a valued contributor to spiritual conversation and prayer, both men and women seemed to want my input and gifts. It was incredibly hard for me to see or understand why.

> *Couldn't they see I was probably just a fake?*
>
> *Didn't they know I wasn't capable of hearing God's voice?*
>
> *Surely they weren't fooled into thinking I had any idea what scripture was talking about!*

And the biggest doubt of all:

> *What if they trust me to make a decision and I THINK I'm following the Holy Spirit but I totally miss it and everyone suffers because I missed it?*

Bit by bit, I began to let my eyes see myself differently. I was like, "Well, these people who seem to be real and honest and humble think the Spirit uses me, so maybe that's true? Maybe I'm not as spiritually crippled as I thought?" I asked God to open my eyes and then I chose to keep them open.

I think of Gideon in Judges 6. In verse 15 Gideon tells God how he sees himself. He's the weakest member of the weakest clan in his tribe. But how did the angel of the Lord greet Gideon in verse 12? "The Lord is with you, O mighty man of valor."

How would you immediately, honestly describe yourself to God right now?

Are you willing to ask God how He sees you? If so, write down what you feel He's saying here:

Take some time to find a couple scriptures you can claim as truth over yourself as you seek to see yourself differently.

Here are a couple of my favorites:

> *I can do all things through him who strengthens me.*
> PHILIPPIANS 4:13

> *No, in all these things we are more than conquerors through him who loved us.*
> ROMANS 8:37

> *I praise you, for I am fearfully and wonderfully made.*
> PSALM 139:14

Do you feel like others see something stronger in you than you've ever believed about yourself?

Write down who sees those things in you and what you think they're seeing.

Do you have a friend who's in the same boat
- a friend who's crippled by insecurity and you know they need to be called out of that cave into abundance?

Write a prayer for them here.

If you feel compelled, set a repeat reminder in your calendar to pray this over that friend once a week.

And now you. Does it seem nobody's seeing the true good in you? Is there no one calling you to something deeper?

Take this space to write a simple prayer, asking God for that kind of person in your life.

Read the next chapter for Step Two.

CHAPTER 20
Look at the Spirit

Step 2: I had to be willing to see the Holy Spirit differently.

This also happened primarily through people. Through a friend, I got connected to a hilarious, Spirit-filled group of ladies who weren't tunnel-vision focusing on the power of the Spirit as much as they focused on the truth of His character and His Word.

Through meeting with them and a mentoring relationship with one of them, I learned this life-changing lesson: "Don't take yourself too seriously, but take God very seriously." As we prayed for each other and for our city, I would see them sometimes knowing exactly what to pray and sometimes having no idea. They were comfortable moving forward in faith, even if they didn't always have a direct "message" from God about what to do.

How did they do this fearlessly?

They were utterly convinced God loves them.

And even if they made a mistake, God would show up in spite of it all. It's a shout out to Romans 8:28 "And we know that for those who love God all things work together for good, for those who are called according to his purpose." And the exclamation point comes shortly thereafter in verses 38-39: "For I am sure that neither death nor life, nor angels nor rulers, nor things present nor things to come, nor powers, nor height nor depth, nor anything else in all creation, will be able to separate us from the love of God in Christ Jesus our Lord."

I wasn't convinced. But they were. And I wanted that. So I began to practice it. Literally.

When I would begin to get frantic about buying the wrong gum at the grocery checkout, I would turn my head away from the gum display and just blindly grab something. (Sometimes that was incredibly disappointing as far as flavor goes, but that wasn't the point.) I would chew the gum and remind myself with something like, "God loves me no matter what kind of gum I chew."

And you know what? It turns out my gum didn't make or break my day.

Taking that a step further, if I was panicking about which way to turn at an intersection, I would intentionally go the way that made me feel the most afraid. As I turned, I would say, "God, I need you to prove that I don't need to be paranoid like that. I need this turn to be okay."

And it was. Although, I was probably often late to various events because I was taking all those wrong turns. Oh well. As my neighbor would say, "It is what it is."

I began to see the Holy Spirit wasn't there to micro-manage the details of my life. I entered into a freedom of knowing the Spirit was in me and adored me and if God needed me to be somewhere, the Spirit would make sure I was there. And I usually didn't even know it was happening. I found I could live my life as a devoted follower of Christ and the Spirit would guide, remind and help me.

Are you feeling frantic and "spiritually superstitious" about a situation right now?

Take time to write a proclamation statement that God's love for you never changes.

CHAPTER 21
Invitation Prayer

My temptation for this section of the book was to teach you all about the scriptures around the Holy Spirit. I quickly realized I was doing that in an attempt to gain your admiration and convince you that I "really know what I'm talking about." Man - will the maturing process ever end? I think not.

When I paused, asking the Lord where to go next, I very simply heard, *Pray*. I responded with a warm, resounding *Yes*!

What follows is a prayer of healing and invitation in your relationship with the Holy Spirit. Before we get there, I want you to consider three things:

1. **Try to schedule an intentional time to pray through this.** Some of you are going to find that easier to do than others. I'm not saying you need to go to a mountaintop by yourself for three days. Just do your best and work within your personal parameters and capabilities.

2. **Let a trusted intercessor know when you're**

going to be praying through this prayer. Ask if they would pray for you at that time against distraction and for a deeper relationship with the Holy Spirit. If you're comfortable, you could invite them to be with you as you pray through it. It's up to you. Either way, I always love knowing I have back up when I'm praying through bigger issues. If you don't have anyone who can fulfill this role, message me through social media or my website telling me when you're praying though this and I'll pray for you.

3. **Don't rush through it.** In fact, I've broken the prayer into different sections so you can pray for a bit, do some processing, take care of some things you need to do, whatever. Then you can get back to it when you have the ability to focus for another block of time.

Okay. Stop. Take a deep breath and let's pray. I would encourage you to pray it out loud, if you are able.

Part One - **Declaration**

Father in Heaven, I'm approaching You because Your Word says I can approach Your throne of grace with confidence and receive mercy and grace to help in my time of need (Hebrews 4:16). I am amazed at how much You love me. Thank You that You have enough love for the entire world (John 3:16)! Your love never ends or runs dry (Psalm 107:1-9). You adopted *me*! The more I realize the weight of that, the more it changes me. I'm humbled that Jesus is my co-heir and willingly shares the love of the Father with me (Romans 8:14-17).

No matter how I feel regarding my earthly dad, I confess that You are love and I abide in Your love (1 John 4:16-18). Right now I need You to hold my hand as I approach my relationship with Your Holy Spirit. I recognize that relationship is broken and I want that to change, but I'm nervous. I don't know if I've fully trusted the Holy Spirit before and I wonder how walking in that trust will affect my life. Psalm 23 reminds me that You are with me everywhere I go and I'm trusting that is true right now - in this moment. Thank You for strengthening me and helping me (Isaiah 41:10) as I take steps towards greater intimacy with Your Spirit.

Is there anything else you want to say or write to the Father? Here is some space to do that, if you like.

Part Two - Confession + Choice

Holy Spirit, my view of You has been distorted.

(choose which prayers are most authentic for you or write your own)

The Word says You are a Helper (John 14:16-17), but I've had a hard time believing that because...

The Word says You will teach me (John 14:26), but I've had a hard time believing that because...

The Bible says there's nowhere I can go that You aren't with me (Psalm 139:7-8), but I've had a hard time believing that because...

The Bible says where You are, there is freedom
(2 Corinthians 3:17), but I've had a hard time
believing that because...

The Word says You are empowering (Acts 1:8), but
I've had a hard time believing that because...

The Bible says You give spiritual gifts (1 Corinthians
12:4-11), but I've not believed that. Instead, I've
had a hard time believing that because...

The Bible says You will guide and direct me (Acts
16:6-10), but I'm scared of that because...

Now take this time to honestly confess any other untruthful things you've believed about the Spirit. Here's my list from chapter 2.

I see Your activity in my life, but I'm not sure I trust You.

Do You just use me to make You look better?

Do You actually know me or do You just appease me?

I see You doing lots of cool things, but I don't think I trust Your motives.

Write yours here and pray through them, confessing honestly to the Lord.

Thank You that I can confess openly to You. It's pointless to keep it covered because You see all the words before they're even on my tongue anyway (Psalm 139:1-4).

And now I choose to believe Your truth rather than my ever-changing feelings. My emotions don't always point towards truth (Jeremiah 17:9). They have misled me in my view of the Spirit. I confess I've followed my emotions into places of doubt and distrust. Thank You that as I confess, I know You are faithful and just to forgive me and cleanse me (1 John 1:9).

For those who would like to write the statement in your own handwriting, there is space after each one to do so.

I choose to believe the Holy Spirit is my Helper.

I choose to believe the Holy Spirit will teach me.

I choose to believe the Holy Spirit is always with me.

I choose to believe that where the Holy Spirit is, there is freedom.

I choose to believe the Holy Spirit is empowering.

I choose to believe the Holy Spirit gives spiritual gifts.

I choose to believe the Holy Spirit will guide and direct me.

I choose to believe the Holy Spirit is trustworthy.

I choose to believe the Holy Spirit is not a controlling tyrant like humans I have known.

I choose to believe the Holy Spirit is not a narcissist.

I choose to believe the Holy Spirit knows me fully.

I choose to believe the Holy Spirit is for me, not against me.

I choose to believe the Holy Spirit was sent by my Father in Heaven.

I choose to believe the Holy Spirit reminds me of Jesus' teachings.

I choose to believe the Holy Spirit is my advocate, not my enemy.

I choose to believe the Holy Spirit is the greatest spirit.

I choose to believe I cannot truly thrive in a fruitful life without the Holy Spirit.

Part Three - **Invitation**

Before praying through this section, I want you to set aside a larger chunk of time for sitting, listening and feeling. Do you have 20 minutes? That's great! Are you able to set aside an hour? Awesome. Just get intentional about making this time quiet and distraction free, not because the Holy Spirit depends on your quietness in order to move or speak. The quiet is for *you*. You have permission to do nothing but sit in God's presence.

Lord, after Jesus resurrected from the dead, Your Word (John 20:22) says "he breathed on them and said to them, 'Receive the Holy Spirit.'" Father, part of me longs for that - for an intimate encounter with Your Spirit. I know Your Spirit dwells in me (1 Corinthians 3:16) but I want more. You've promised "If you then, who are evil, know how to give good gifts to your children, how much more will the heavenly Father give the Holy Spirit to those who ask him!" (Luke 11:13).

And then I think about the scripture that says You are "able to do immeasurably more than all we ask or imagine" (Ephesians 3:20) and I am compelled to say, "I want that. I want more. Even though it makes me nervous and a little scared, I do want more of Your Spirit."

I belong to Christ Jesus and the passions and desires of my sinful nature have been nailed to His cross and they are crucified there. I choose living by the Spirit! Help me to follow Your leading in every part of my life. Holy Spirit, I know You produce love, self-control, joy, faithfulness, goodness, patience, kindness, gentleness, and peace in my life and I anticipate more of that as I surrender daily to You and continually seek Your filling (Galatians 5:22-25).

I don't want to be like some sort of lifeless statue, having a mouth that doesn't speak, having eyes that cannot see, having ears that can't hear and having a mouth that doesn't truly breathe (Psalm 135: 15-18). Holy Spirit, awaken and ignite my senses! Open my mouth wide with Your powerful words, truth, and praise! Uncover my eyes to see things they've never noticed before! Unplug my ears so I can hear You fully and intimately! Fill my lungs with *Your* breath and *Your* life!

Today I'm putting a stake in the ground.

Holy Spirit, I want more of You.

I know You are in me and I want MORE of You.

Fill me until there's room for nothing but You!

I want to overflow with You!

In You I live and move and exist (Acts 17:28).

Fill me.

Fill me.

Fill *me*.

I invite You to fill me.

Now give yourself some time and space to connect with what the Holy Spirit is doing. Lay down, sit down, dance...whatever feels most important in this moment.

Don't think of this as some sort of mystical experience where if you say the right things and do the right things, the Holy Spirit will show up. No. This is like a holy date - time for you and the Holy Spirit to get reacquainted without any distractions.

Focus on the Lord and record any thoughts, pictures, words, feelings and reactions you experience here, no matter how insignificant they may seem. Write down any scriptures, worship songs and lyrics that come to mind, too.

Here are some writing prompts that may help you.

I feel... I know... I see... I sense... I hear... I'm thinking... I remember... I'm aware... I think the Spirit is giving me this spiritual gift... I'm thinking about this scripture...

Before you enter into this time, I want you to lay down your expectations. Many times when I invite the Holy Spirit's presence, I don't necessarily *feel* anything. But that does not mean He's abandoned me or isn't present. Remember how Psalm 139:7-8 tells us He's always with us. Just make your undistracted self available.

Here's some space for you to record, write or draw anything that comes to mind.

A closing prayer:

Holy Spirit, thank You that I know You are with me, whether I feel it or not. Thank You that I am never truly alone because You are with me. I love You and want to continually grow in trusting You. Thank You for empowering me to be a mother.

In the name of Jesus, Amen.

Here are some things I wrote down after doing this myself:

I feel hopeful.

I'm aware of the Spirit's presence.

I can breathe deeply.

I am weepy and happy all at once.

I'm aware that He can't be controlled, not because He's afraid of being controlled, but because He just literally can't be. There is nothing or no one who has the ability to control the Spirit - and that makes me trust Him even more somehow.

Remember, if you didn't "feel" or "experience" anything specific or mind-blowing during your time. **It's okay.** As we said earlier, we can't let our opinion of the Spirit be based on our emotions. We have to trust He is there and He is present and listening, even if we don't feel anything at all.

Schedule time to make this sort of invitation prayer a regular part of your life until it becomes a natural part of your relationship with the Holy Spirit.

Keep believing. Keep choosing. Keep pursuing. Keep asking. (Luke 11:9-13)

PART SIX

The
Transformation

CHAPTER 22
Get Your Labeling Gun

We just celebrated Easter a week ago. To remind myself of the details surrounding Christ's crucifixion, I read through it in the Gospel of Matthew. Having been a follower of Christ for over 30 years, I'd read this many times. But isn't it amazing when something you've read a gazillion times suddenly becomes NEW? God's Word is like that.

As I read about Jesus giving up his last human breath, I was moved by a new revelation.

Here's Matthew 27:50-54 for your reference:

And Jesus cried out again with a loud voice and yielded up his spirit. And behold, the curtain of the temple was torn in two, from top to bottom. And the earth shook, and the rocks were split. The tombs also were opened. And many bodies of the saints who had fallen asleep were raised, and coming out of the tombs after his resurrection they went into the holy city and appeared to many. When the centurion and those who were

*with him, keeping watch over Jesus, saw the
earthquake and what took place, they were
filled with awe and said, "Truly this was the Son
of God!"*
MATTHEW 27:50-54

The centurion (an officer in the Roman army)
and those who were with him were watching
Jesus like it was their *job*! Okay. It actually *was*
their job. No matter the reason, their eyes were
fixed on Jesus. And because of that, they were
transformed! Because they were watching Jesus,
they immediately saw the connection between His
last breath and the rocks splitting, tombs opening,
and earth quaking. Those who weren't watching
him would have been more likely to miss the
transforming truth: *Jesus is the Son of God!*

While others who didn't believe went on their
way, back to their homes and normal lives, the
centurion was changed because his eyes were on
Jesus.

Does that sound hyper-spiritual? Maybe too
nebulous to actually comprehend? *How do you
keep your eyes on Jesus?*

Maybe an obvious answer is: Read and study the

Bible. And that's true. It's critical to walking in truth and wholeness. John 1:14 tells us Jesus was the Word in flesh living with us. When we study the Word, we are truly keeping our eyes on Jesus.

Another way I'm attempting to keep my eyes on Jesus is to turn my eyes away from "not Jesus." You could even say it like that, as if Not Jesus is a label you put on things like a sticker on a package.

Watching a TV show and the Holy Spirit's like, "Um. No." You can say out loud, "Oh, hey! That's Not Jesus." On to better things.

Reading a book and you're really into it but it's taking a dark turn and you can see it moving towards something bad for your brain. Not Jesus. Get rid of the book.

Listening to a podcast and, man, that girl is fiery and inspiring! And yet, she's *really* driving home messages that *kind of* sound like the Bible but it's not quite *right*. Not Jesus. Moving on...

What things in your life need to have a Not Jesus label placed on them?

And as we watch Jesus Christ of Nazareth who died and rose again, we must allow ourselves to be transformed, just like the centurion. He could have resisted the transformation. He could have dismissed the truth. Instead, he allowed his mouth to speak new words.

Give yourself permission to speak and believe truth. God's truth. Maybe that sounds weird, but some of us have been believing the same things about ourselves and God for so long we can feel really uncomfortable believing something different - even it's a better, healthier thing to believe!

When the Bible says God has good plans for you (Jeremiah 29:11), choose to have confidence in that.

When the Bible says you are chosen and adopted by God (Romans 8:14-17), choose to live that way.

When the Bible says fearing the Lord is more glorious than physical beauty (Proverbs 31:30), choose to let that actually affect your decisions and thoughts.

And so on and so on.

CHAPTER 23
Arise, Mother!

Sitting across the table from a new friend at our local breakfast restaurant, we swapped tattoo stories. We talked about big things and little things. It was a rich conversation, like a deep well of refreshment. I realized I have another sister in Christ who I adore. In the midst of a conversation about motherhood as she was preparing to bring a sweet baby into her life through adoption, she dropped a scripture that made the whole room go silent around me. I felt it in my actual *bones*.

It's from a song written out in Judges 5, verse 7, specifically:

> *I, Deborah, arose as a mother in Israel.*

She arose as a mother.

The next thought in my mind was, "I think that's what I'm doing. I'm arising as a mother! A strong, powerful, warrior mother."

Deborah was a prophetess. She actually had her

own tree, under which she would sit while people came to her for wisdom and help (Judges 4:5).

At this time Israel was in captivity and God told Deborah the plan for rescue. Did you hear that? God told a *woman* the plan! I love it.

The whole story is amazing, culminating in another mighty woman, Jael, driving a tent peg through the bad guy's head. So there's that.

After all was said and done and Israel was free again, Deborah and Baraak (the guy who lead the army against the captors) sang a song (Judges 6).

Side note: How in the world did that work? Did they sit and write it down, decide on a melody and go for it? Was it just entirely Spirit-inspired? Did the song happen months afterwards so they had time to consult their local songwriter? Another question on my list of Things to Ask in Heaven...

Regardless of how the song came about, it includes a beautiful line of Deborah rising up as a mother for Israel.

> A woman who saw what needed to be done and did it.

> A woman who heard from God and spoke it.

A woman who wasn't afraid to lead.

A woman who saw captives and determined to set them free.

A woman who wasn't afraid to let *another* woman get the glory of finally defeating the enemy.

A woman who moved away from her comfy tree and headed into battle.

A woman who wasn't afraid to be a mother.

I have goosebumps all over my arms after writing that out.

Deborah arose as a mother when she went to battle.

Our children are like arrows. Weapons in a warrior's hands.

When God gives you arrows, you rise and go to battle.

When we arise as mothers, and release our arrows into their purpose, we are warriors.

Warrior mothers.

Yes, Lord. Make us warrior mothers!

What is your reaction to the story of Deborah arising as a mother?

In the midst of your writing, you may have found yourself thinking or saying, "I want that!"

And here's the thing: **You have it.**

You have everything you need to rise as a mother with honor, strength, dignity, purpose and joy.

You have it because, if you are a follower of Christ, the Spirit is in you - empowering, reminding, and teaching you (1 Corinthians 3:16).

It may not happen overnight. In fact, it likely will take some time. But it will happen.

Let's pray.

Lord, I want to arise as a mother.

A mother for my children.

A mother for my church.

A mother for my neighborhood.

A mother for anyone in my path who needs the nurturing of God.

I submit myself to Your teaching and guidance.

I give myself permission to change.

Holy Spirit, I invite You to transform me. Teach me to stand as the woman I was created to be.

Make me a warrior mother.

Amen and amen.

Many Thanks!

Holy Spirit, without You, I would be homeless, directionless, powerless. With You, I know who I am. With You, I'm never alone. **With You, I am a Warrior Mother.**

Lucy, as our first born arrow, you had such an immature mom for quite a while. Thanks for all of the grace. I'm so proud of your honesty, your simple faith, your heart for justice and your determination.

Eve, I'm so glad you became our arrow when you were 9. I know the word "mother" hasn't always been a source of comfort for you. But I'm so proud of how you choose love and trust for me as your mom. Your strength shines like the sun.

And Jack, our youngest arrow, your name means "God's grace" and that is truly what you extend with the greatest of ease. Thanks for being a hugger with me. You are an amazing young man.

Well, Andy. Instead of typing something out, it would be much easier for me to just sit and cry. Wait. I need to sit and cry for a minute.

Okay. I'm ready.

Andy, when I met you at the water fountain in 7th grade, I could not have possibly dreamed of where we are now. I adore you. Your belief in me makes me so uncomfortable. And I'm so grateful for it. May our home always be a lighthouse.

Fran, from the moment I married your son, you called me Daughter and never looked back.

Mom, even though I can't really explain how I know, I know you're happy with this book. And that makes me smile.

Thank you Jon Stube Ph. D, LPC, Suzy Weibel, Reverend Jonathan Srock, Ambri Heimerman, Pastor Jarrod Sechler, Pastor Jonathan Weibel, Courtney Bullard and Laura Booz for reading this book when it was in its most raw state.

I've had the most amazing supportive friends throughout this process. Ambri Heimerman, Steph Banks, Liz Helland, Alyssa Good and the rest of the Psalm 40 group, Colette Heinz, Ashley McDonald, Nancy Stormer, Laura Booz, Anne Yorks, Dannah Gresh and the rest of the DR Ladies, Suzy Weibel, Chizuruoke Anderson, Hannah Nitz, my DC group, the women of Centre Church...a whole bunch of powerful women who speak truth and fight for freedom. Dree Hogue, thank you for teaching me the true definition of friendship. I'm forever thankful that you didn't give up on me.

Ginger, thank you for changing my life with one simple challenge.

ABOUT THE AUTHOR
Janet Mylin

Hi, there! I'm Janet.
By the grace of God,
I wrote this book and
hope to write more
as the Spirit leads and
directs.

If you're curious about
what I'm up to, my website is a great place to start.

Go to *janetmylin.com* for

- my podcast
- speaking videos
- free downloads

And more!

You can also have fun with me over in the land of
Instagram. *@janetmylin*

Wanna talk? Go ahead and either DM me via
Instagram or send me an email via my website.

OTHER BOOKS BY JANET MYLIN

The One Year Mother- Daughter Devo

by Dannah Gresh with Janet Mylin

This book was designed to help you spend fun, interesting and connective time in the Word with your tween daughter. *Over 90,000 copies sold!*

www.tyndale.com/kids

Just Call Me Kate

by Dannah Gresh and Janet Mylin

Kate has a bad case of "Boy Craziness." Through a caring teacher and a few new friends, she realizes there's more for her than just crushing on boys.

www.moodypublishers.com